Airport
Twentieth Century in Pictures

Airport

Twentieth Century in Pictures

AMMONITE
PRESS

**PRESS
ASSOCIATION**
Images

First Published 2009 by
Ammonite Press
an imprint of AE Publications Ltd,
166 High Street, Lewes, East Sussex BN7 1XU

ISBN 978-1-906672-31-7

British Cataloguing in Publication Data. A catalogue
record of this book is available from the British Library.

Editor: Richard Wiles
Series Editor: Paul Richardson
Picture research: Press Association Images
Design: Gravemaker + Scott

Colour reproduction by GMC Reprographics
Printed by Kyodo Nation Printing Services Co., Ltd.

Page 2: Prior to his
departure for America,
Charlie Chaplin flew to Paris
from Croydon Aerodrome
in *The City of London*,
the Vickers Vimy biplane
G-EASI, operated by Instone
Air Line, which flew mail
between the cities.
5th October, 1921

Page 5: John, Paul, George
and Ringo, home after their
successful American tour,
wave enthusiastically to
the hordes of screaming
teenagers who had
assembled at Heathrow
Airport to greet them.
22nd February, 1964

Page 6: Midge Ure, 31, of
the rock group Ultravox,
who with Bob Geldof wrote
the Band Aid single *Do
They Know It's Christmas?*
spraying a message
on a water tanker at
Gatwick Airport.
9th March, 1985

Introduction

In the days when life seemed – at least to our modern eyes – to proceed at a more stately pace, those with the means and inclination to leave the British Isles would do so by sea: thus the hubs of international passenger travel were great ports such as Liverpool and Southampton. Such was the length of a sea voyage in those times that the departure and arrival of a passenger liner was newsworthy; passenger lists were eagerly scanned by journalists who would diligently report the comings and goings of the great and the good.

But as the 20th century progressed, life's pace quickened and air travel supplanted ocean crossings. The first Air Port of London, the capital's official point of entry and departure for international flights, was Croydon Airport – or 'Aerodrome', as it was originally described. Opened in 1920, it offered scheduled services to Paris, Amsterdam and Rotterdam, adding Berlin in 1923. Travel by these services was not for the faint-hearted: one traveller described his experience in less-than glowing terms: "*They put you in a box, they shut the lid, they splash you all over with oil, you are sick, and you're in Paris*". After the Second World War, airliners were more sophisticated, comfortable and most of all larger: too large, in fact, for Croydon's limited runway space, and in 1946 its prestigious status as 'London Airport' was lost to Heathrow.

In those post-war years air travel was unquestionably the sophisticated way to arrive and leave: and the great and good, whose sea voyages were once the subject of journalistic interest, gratified the newspapers still further by popping in and out of airports as if they were revolving doors. The Press Association, Britain's news agency since the 19th century, dutifully stationed photographers in the lounges of Heathrow and Gatwick as they had once manned the quays of Southampton and Liverpool, recording the arrivals and departures of those rarified individuals possessing that intangible but unmistakable quality: celebrity.

As a collection, the photographs reproduced here give a fascinating insight into the nature of celebrity in Britain, and how it has changed over the years. Or has it? Film stars, pop singers, sportsmen and women, politicians and royalty are as prominent today as they were in the 1950s. But it is hard to imagine a 1960s chef attracting photographers' attention in the same way that Gordon Ramsay does today: perhaps this is the exception that proves the rule.

Facing page: American aviator Captain Charles Lindbergh at Croydon Airport, South London on his way to Southampton, a week after his record breaking non-stop flight from New York to Paris in the single-engine, single-seat monoplane *Spirit of St Louis*. At Southampton the *USS Memphis* took Lindbergh to Washington, USA, where President Calvin Coolidge awarded him the Distinguished Flying Cross.

28th May, 1927

American singing and film star, Tony Martin and his wife, ballerina turned actress and dancer Cyd Charisse on a flying visit to London, shortly after their marriage. In one of Hollywood's strongest pairings, the couple would remain happily married for almost 60 years, until Charisse's death in 2008. Martin continued to tour at the age of 96.

4th June, 1948

Clutching a bouquet of flowers, Ingrid Bergman smiles farewell to fans as she leaves Northolt Airport after a visit to Britain, just weeks before the US release of Victor Fleming's film *Joan of Arc*, in which she played the eponymous heroine, reprising her stage performance in the Broadway play *Joan of Lorraine*.
5th October, 1948

Joe E Brown, Hollywood film actor and comedian, arrives at London Heathrow Airport. He was to take the leading role of affable Elwood P Dowd in *Harvey,* Mary Coyle Chase's comedy about a man's relationship with an imaginary *"six-foot, three-and-one-half-inch tall"* rabbit, at the Prince of Wales theatre in London, while Sid Field took a month's holiday.
23rd August, 1949

British film star Jean Simmons boards a Pan American Clipper for America at Heathrow Airport, the year she was to marry actor Stewart Granger and make the transition to Hollywood. Simmons became an Officer of the Order of the British Empire (OBE) in the New Year's Honours List in 2003.

7th December, 1950

Actor Humphrey Bogart, his actress wife Lauren Bacall (L) and actress Katharine Hepburn (R) at Heathrow Airport, after arriving from Africa. Bogart and Hepburn had been filming John Huston's *The African Queen* for four months. Bacall had joined them for the duration, leaving her young child behind, and acted as cook, nurse and clothes washer.
18th July, 1951

Orson Welles, the American author, actor and producer, leaves Heathrow Airport for Rome, towards the end of filming *Othello*. Welles not only wrote the screenplay based on Shakespeare's play, but also produced and directed, while taking the lead role.

30th August, 1951

Denis Compton, Middlesex and England cricketer, who
played in 78 test matches, and who jointly captained
Middlesex CCC with W J Edrich between 1951 and 1952,
boards a plane at Heathrow Airport bound for South Africa.
4th October, 1951

British singer, actor and comedian Norman Wisdom performs for a crowd at Heathrow Airport after arriving back from New York, where he had scored a success on US television. Initially straight man to magician David Nixon, Wisdom's rise to fame was rapid, and he became a West End star within two years of his debut performance at 31.

5th December, 1951

Dressed in black Queen Elizabeth II sets foot on British soil for the first time since her accession to the throne, landing at Heathrow Airport after a gruelling day and night flight from Kenya following the death of her father, King George VI.

7th February, 1952

Facing page: American actor Charlton Heston, debonair star of Cecil de Mille's *The Greatest Show on Earth* pictured with his 28 year old actress wife Lydia Heston at Heathrow Airport. The movie, in which Heston played a big top circus manager, won an Oscar for Best Picture at the 25th Academy Awards.

17th March, 1952

Rock Hudson, seen arriving at Heathrow from his native United States, was a relatively unknown actor just four years previously, until his good looks earned him broader recognition, and he became one of the most popular romantic leading men of the day in movies and on television.

11th August, 1952

Charlie Chaplin and his wife, Oona, preparing to leave Heathrow Airport for Paris. It had just been announced by US Attorney-General James P McGranery in Washington that Chaplin – under investigation by the FBI and the House Un-American Activities Commission for his left-wing leanings, and refused re-entry to the USA the previous month – would be allowed to re-enter America only if he could prove his 'worth and right'. He chose not to.
29th October, 1952

Facing page: Hollywood actress Ava Gardner with her husband, the singer Frank Sinatra, at Heathrow Airport on the first stage of their journey to Nairobi for location work on Miss Gardner's new film *Mogambo*.
6th November, 1952

Facing page: Nattily dressed Hollywood Oscar-winning actor Humphrey Bogart looks relaxed and happy after flying to London Heathrow from New York.
17th January, 1953

Peter Lorre, the Hungarian-Austrian American born László Löwenstein, a mild-mannered man frequently typecast in screen roles as a sinister foreigner, arrives at Heathrow Airport by Pan American Clipper en route for Rome, where he was to co-star with Humphrey Bogart in John Huston's film *Beat the Devil*.
12th February, 1953

Walt Disney, multiple Academy Award-winning American film producer, director, screenwriter, animator, entrepreneur and philanthropist – and the man behind the voice of the inimitable cartoon character Mickey Mouse – arrives at Heathrow Airport bound for the United States.
11th April, 1953

Facing page: Elegant Belgian-born actress Audrey Hepburn arrives at Heathrow Airport from New York, shortly before the release of the film *Roman Holiday*, in which she starred alongside Gregory Peck and subsequently won the Academy Award for Best Actress.
21st May, 1953

Stepping from a BOAC airliner at Heathrow Airport, (L–R) Edmund Hillary of New Zealand, the Nepalese-Tibetan Sherpa Tenzing Norgay, and flag-waving Colonel John Hunt received a rapturous welcome, after the expedition had been first to reach the summit of Mount Everest.
3rd July, 1953

In stylish pattern contrast coat, radiant English-born
American film star Elizabeth Taylor arrives with actor
husband Michael Wilding at Heathrow Airport after a holiday
in Rome. Wilding was the second of Taylor's eventual eight
marriages (including twice to actor Richard Burton).
16th September, 1953

Major American box office star, Clark Gable, pictured before boarding a KLM plane at London Heathrow Airport. Unhappy with what he considered mediocre roles offered to him by MGM – while the studio regarded his salary as excessive – Gable refused to renew his contract in 1953 and began to work independently.
23rd September, 1953

English-born American entertainer Bob Hope, pictured at Heathrow Airport after a flying visit to Madrid, Spain, holds aloft a souvenir, jocularly called 'Crosby' in reference to his long-time partner Bing.
1st October, 1953

Hollywood actress Ginger Rogers, 42, and her fourth
husband Frenchman Jacques Bergerac, 26, at Heathrow
Airport on their arrival from Paris. They were to appear in
Miss Rogers' first British film *Lifeline* for Marksman Films, in
which she was to play an American actress who falls in love
with a young Frenchman (played by her husband).
25th November, 1953

Master of suspense and psychological thrillers, British-born Hollywood film director Alfred Hitchcock is pictured at Heathrow Airport as he was about to board a BEA plane for Paris.

13th May, 1954

Prior to his notoriety in a string of Hammer horror films, English actor Peter Cushing had worked mainly in theatre and television. He is seen here with his wife, actress Helen Beck, at Heathrow Airport on their return by BEA airliner from Madrid.
6th June, 1955

Despite screen roles such as Frankenstein's monster in numerous horror films, Boris Karloff – born William Henry Pratt, from East Dulwich, London – was known to be a kind, generous man, characteristics that are revealed in this smiling portrait shot at Heathrow Airport after the actor had arrived on a Pan American Clipper from the United States.
2nd September, 1955

English crime writer and playwright Agatha Christie, 65, and her grandson, Mathew Prichard, leave Heathrow Airport to spend Christmas in Tripoli. On the novelist's death in 1976 Prichard became heir to much of his grandmother's literary work, including her famous play *The Mousetrap*.
21st December, 1955

Sir Laurence and Lady Olivier (L and second L) were at
Heathrow Airport to meet Marilyn Monroe (third L) and her
husband, playwright Arthur Miller (R), on their arrival from
New York. Marilyn is to co-star with Sir Laurence in the film
The Sleeping Prince, which is to be made at Pinewood.
14th July, 1956

Film stars David Niven (L), Ava Gardner and Stewart Granger embarked on a flight from Heathrow Airport to Rome, where they were to film scenes from the comedy film *The Little Hut*.

22nd July, 1956

Facing page: Comedy actor Peter Sellers and his wife Anne waiting at London Heathrow Airport for a flight to New York. They were on their way to Toronto, Canada, where Sellers appeared on television.

27th November, 1956

A straw hat was worn by the photographer Cecil Beaton at Heathrow Airport. He was flying to New York on the way to Dallas, USA to be presented with the Neiman-Marcus Award for distinguished service to fashion, as a result of his work for the stage show *My Fair Lady*.

29th August, 1956

British radio and television comedian Tony Hancock in high spirits as he boards a BEA Elizabethan Class plane at Heathrow Airport, bound for Paris on a short holiday.
29th January, 1957

Effervescent cabaret star Shirley Bassey, wearing a distinctive new hairstyle, arrives at Heathrow Airport from New York. The British singer was enjoying a Top Ten hit in the UK with *Banana Boat Song*, and had also recorded in the US under the direction of Mitch Miller at Columbia Records.
19th April, 1957

Facing page: Film star Diana Dors, who had filed a divorce petition against her husband, Dennis Hamilton, was pictured with actor Tommy Yeardye before they left Heathrow Airport for Rome. While performing as a body double for actor Victor Mature, 6ft 4in Yeardye was obliged to embrace Dors, and the pair began a relationship shortly afterwards.
2nd July, 1957

Film actress Sylvia Syms leaves Heathrow Airport for Berlin to attend the Film Festival, in which her movie *Woman in a Dressing Gown* is being shown as the official British entry. Miss Syms co-stars with Anthony Quayle and Yvonne Mitchell in the film.
1st July, 1957

Tommy Steele, Britain's first teen idol and rock 'n' roll star, at Heathrow Airport before leaving for Copenhagen at the start of a two week personal appearance tour, which would take in Stockholm, Oslo, Hamburg and Brussels. The visits were in connection with the release of his new film *The Tommy Steele Story* in those cities.

5th September, 1957

Television game show host Hughie Green sits at the piano and is joined in song by siffleur Ronnie Ronalde and singer Rosalina Neri aboard a BOAC Britannia aircraft at Heathrow Airport. They were rehearsing for a flight to New York, which would be filmed as *Jack Hylton's Monday Show* for screening on ITV. Neri had been involved in a much-publicised volatile relationship with bandleader Hylton.

28th January, 1958

Italian actress Sophia Loren and her film producer husband Carlo Ponti arrive at Heathrow Airport from Paris. Ponti had obtained a Mexican divorce in 1957 from first wife Giuliana, and married Loren by proxy, although since divorce was forbidden in Italy risked a charge of bigamy should he return to Italy. Eight years later, as French citizens, they remarried legally in Sèvres.

27th May, 1958

French actress Brigitte Bardot at Heathrow Airport, after arriving from Paris to start location shooting of her latest movie *Babette Goes to War*.
9th April, 1959

American singer and entertainer Eddie Fisher and his wife, film star Elizabeth Taylor, on arrival at Heathrow Airport, from a holiday in Nice.
19th July, 1959

Tommy Steele performs a traditional Russian dance on the tarmac at Heathrow Airport, on his arrival from Moscow.

8th August, 1959

American 'Blonde Bombshell' actress Jayne Mansfield, pictured with her Hungarian husband Mickey Hargitay, actor and Mr Universe 1955, Mansfield's nine year old daughter Jayne Marie (from her previous marriage) and the couple's 11 month old son Miklós at Heathrow Airport.

16th December, 1959

American singer Ella Fitzgerald arriving at Heathrow Airport, from Paris. Fitzgerald is in the country to top the bill during the British tour of the American show *Jazz at the Philharmonic* at the Royal Festival Hall in London.

4th March, 1960

Facing page: Greek shipping magnate and millionaire Aristotle Onassis, whose wife, Tina, had just obtained an American divorce, arrives at Heathrow Airport. His affair with opera diva Maria Callas while both parties were otherwise married had received much publicity in the popular press.
28th June, 1960

The Andrews Sisters, billed as the world's most successful close-harmony singing group, are seen arriving at Heathrow Airport from New York to appear at *Talk of the Town* for an eight week run.
30 November, 1960

Four year old Nicholas Paget-Brown of Esher, Surrey, enjoys
a preview at Heathrow Airport of the Christmas festivities
arranged aboard BOAC jetliners, with a visit from Father
Christmas played by John Alcock of BOAC.
23 December, 1960

Dean Martin (L) and
Frank Sinatra (R) greet
onlookers as they stride
across the Heathrow Airport
tarmac, before travelling to
Shepperton Studios to film
a two minute cameo in
Bing Crosby and Bob
Hope's comedy film *Road
To Hong Kong*.
4th August, 1961

Facing page: Pop singer Cliff Richard (C) poses with members of his supporting instrumental band The Shadows, (L–R) Tony Meehan, Bruce Welch, Hank Marvin and Jet Harris at Heathrow Airport as they are about to fly off on their Scandinavian Tour.
15th August, 1961

American actor Jack Lemmon at Heathrow Airport before leaving for New York. Lemmon was known principally for his comedic roles, in particular the 1959 hit *Some Like it Hot* in which he and Tony Curtis evade gangsters by concealing themselves as women in an all-girl band, which includes the delectable Marilyn Monroe.
12th November, 1961

Facing page: Over a glass of milk and a cigarette, actor Peter O'Toole has a farewell chat with his actress wife Sian Phillips at Heathrow Airport, where he was leaving for Madrid to work on his new film *Lawrence of Arabia*.
13th December, 1961

Hollywood actress Natalie Wood is pictured with suave actor Warren Beatty at Heathrow Airport. The couple, romantically linked, had recently filmed *Splendor in the Grass*, for which Wood received an Oscar nomination for Best Actress.
17th May, 1962

these flights
elephone below.

these flights
ppropriate Airline
this floor.

Facing page: Queen Elizabeth with Princess Margaret and corgis, arriving at Heathrow Airport aboard an RAF Transport Command Comet from Scotland, after a visit to Balmoral Castle.
19 October, 1962

French fashion designer Yves Saint Laurent with his associate Mme Therond, well known as the model Victoire (L) and Mme De Peyerimhoff (R), a manager of his salon, on arrival at Heathrow Airport.
8th October, 1962

Facing page: The legendary Bette Davis and her 16 year old daughter, Barbara, known as 'BD', at Heathrow Airport before leaving for Brussels. Daughter of Davis and the artist William Sherry, BD married film executive Jeremy Hyman the same year, the pairing receiving her mother's public consent. Davis later clashed with her daughter, when BD – now pastor of her own ministry – published two books highly critical of her mother.
10th May, 1963

Christine Keeler, the London model who failed to appear as a witness in an Old Bailey case connected with the Profumo Affair, arrives at Heathrow Airport from Paris and is detained by police. The scandal surrounding Keeler's affair with John Profumo, Secretary of State for War, while she was also sleeping with Yevgeny Ivanov, naval attaché at the Soviet embassy, discredited the Conservative government of Harold Macmillan.
28th March, 1963

Bubbly Barbara Windsor waves farewell on leaving Heathrow Airport for her first visit to America. The comedy film *Sparrers Can't Sing*, in which she co-starred with James Booth, a view of Cockney life in the London's East End during the 1960s, baffled reviewers on its US release, who were unable to comprehend the dialog of rhyming slang, Yiddish and thieves' cant.

26th June, 1963

Nat King Cole with his wife
Maria and four year old son
Nat Kelly Cole on arrival at
London's Heathrow Airport,
where the jazz singer and
pianist was to perform his
first British tour since 1954.
11th July, 1963

Facing page: Four thousand fans of The Beatles descend on Heathrow Airport to greet the 'Fab Four' on their return from their first tour of the United States.
21st February, 1964

Boarding a Pan American airliner at Heathrow Airport as they set off for Australia, are pop groups Gerry and the Pacemakers, the Tremeloes and the Echoes, plus singer Dusty Springfield.
31st March, 1964

Facing page: Rolling Stone Keith Richard (L) and the group's manager Andrew Loog Oldham (R), relax at Heathrow Airport before the band were to leave for a concert in New York, USA.
23rd October, 1964

A pop icon of the 'swinging London' era of the 1960s, British actress Julie Christie waits to board a flight to Madrid, Spain, for a well earned holiday. Miss Christie rose to fame as Tom Courtenay's co-star in *Billy Liar*, as an amoral model in *Darling*, and as mistress of *Doctor Zhivago*, played by Omar Sharif, in the soon to be released film.
13th September, 1964

Facing page: Dressed for a British November rather than a sunny Californian shore are The Beach Boys, the American pop group with the 'surfing' sound, who had arrived at Heathrow Airport from New York by BOAC airliner. The band, (L–R) Carl Wilson, Al Jardine, Dennis Wilson, Brian Wilson and Mike Love were paying their first visit to Britain for a week's radio and television dates to promote their new record release *When I Grow Up (To Be A Man)*.
1st November, 1964

Nobel Peace Prize winner Dr Martin Luther King, who had spent the weekend in London, arrives at Heathrow Airport for a flight to Oslo, Norway, to receive the Nobel Prize for Peace on the 10th of December, 1964. Dr King was the youngest recipient of the award since its inception in 1901.
8th December, 1964

Facing page: British pop singer Sandie Shaw, carrying mascot 'Ossie', poses with singer and actor Adam Faith – who had discovered her when she appeared on the bill at a concert after coming second in a talent contest. The couple are pictured at Heathrow Airport after flying in from Montreal.
29th March, 1965

Dressed in the height of pop fashion, The Beatles arrive at Heathrow Airport en route to the USA: (L–R) Paul McCartney, John Lennon, Ringo Starr and George Harrison.
12th January, 1965

Jackie Kennedy, holding the hand of her son, John Jr, smiles as she walks from the US Presidential aircraft after landing at Heathrow Airport. She has flown over with her two children to attend the unveiling by the Queen of a memorial to her assassinated husband, President John F Kennedy.
12th May, 1965

American jazz pianist, bandleader and composer, Count Basie arrives at Heathrow Airport from Munich, with his orchestra, where he is to appear at the Hammersmith Odeon and Croydon's Fairfield Hall.
18th September, 1965

Wintry London gets a warm greeting from Italian actress Sophia Loren as, in a spotted fur coat and fur hat, she steps from an aircraft at Heathrow Airport after flying in from Paris, followed by her husband, film producer Carlo Ponti. Miss Loren is to make a film with Marlon Brando, the comedy *A Countess from Hong Kong*, the last film directed by Charlie Chaplin, and his only colour film.

15th January, 1966

American bandleader
Duke Ellington and singer
Ella Fitzgerald arriving at
Heathrow Airport. The pair
were in the Britain for a short
tour that began at the Royal
Festival Hall in London.
12th February, 1966

Actress Sharon Tate leaving Heathrow Airport for Munich en route for Northern Italy to work on the film *The Fearless Vampire Killers*, directed by and starring Roman Polanski, who Miss Tate was to marry two years later before her murder in 1969 by followers of the notorious Charles Manson.
23rd February, 1966

Manchester United footballer George Best wearing a souvenir sombrero on his return to Heathrow Airport following the team's defeat of Benfica 5-1 in the second leg of the European Cup quarter final football match. Best scored United's first two goals.

11th March, 1966

Facing page: Prime Minister of India Indira Gandhi breaks her journey from Washington, USA to meet the British Prime Minister Harold Wilson at Heathrow Airport.
4th April, 1966

Wearing his trademark tinted prescription sunglasses, American pop singer Roy Orbison arrives at Heathrow Airport. The eyewear came about when Orbison left his clear glasses on a plane during a tour, and the sunglasses were the only prescription lenses available.
18th March, 1966

Facing page: A farewell wave to Britain from world heavyweight boxing champion Muhammad Ali as he leaves Heathrow Airport for Egypt, where he is to be a guest of the Higher Council for Islamic Affairs. Ali changed his name from Cassius Clay in 1964 after joining the Nation of Islam.
24th May, 1966

The Rolling Stones – (L–R) Mick Jagger, Brian Jones, Bill Wyman, Keith Richards, and (foreground) Charlie Watts – boarding a plane at Heathrow Airport before leaving for America, three days after the US release of *Aftermath*. The album was their first to be recorded entirely in the US at RCA Studios in Hollywood, the first to be released in stereo, and the first consisting entirely of Jagger-Richards compositions.
23rd June, 1966

Jumping for joy at Heathrow Airport is Peter Blaine Noone, better known as Herman of the pop group Herman's Hermits. He was leaving Britain with the band on a six-week tour of America.

27th June, 1966

Brigitte Bardot gives an interview to the press upon her arrival at Heathrow Airport, having flown from Paris to shoot location scenes for the film *Two Weeks in September*; the story of a young French woman married to a much older Englishman, who then falls in love with a younger man.

2nd September, 1966

Wearing dazzle-striped mini skirts, white sweaters and boots,
TV's Beat Girls dance troupe – (L–R) Dee-Dee Wilde, Lorelly
Harris, Diana South, Babs Lord, Penny Fergusson and Felicity
Colby – 'take off' at Heathrow Airport, before leaving for Venice
with The Luvvers pop group. They were to perform at a lavish
party planned by Universal Pictures after the premiere of
Fahrenheit 451, British entry at the Venice Film Festival.
7th September, 1966

Leslie Hornby, the model 'Twiggy' at Heathrow Airport before a journey to Tunisia. When discovered at the age of 16 she weighed only 6½ stone and became 'The Face of '66' after pictures taken by Barry Lategan were released. Her short haired, large-eyed androgynous look changed the world of fashion. Although the look was much mimicked, her slender frame was the result of anorexia, diagnosed at the age of 14.
28th September, 1966

Facing page: Raquel Welch arrives at Heathrow Airport from Malaga, where she starred with Anthony Franciosa in the adventure film *Fathom*, playing the unlikely role of a dental assistant and skydiver hired to recover an atomic triggering device.
18th November, 1966

Identically dressed, the Beverley Sisters pose at Heathrow Airport before leaving for Madrid, where they were to perform their singing act on Spanish television.
1st December, 1966

Fashion designer Mary Quant leaving Heathrow Airport, heading for Amsterdam to judge a mini skirt competition.
16th December, 1966

Coal miner's son and Welsh singing star Tom Jones carries a portable wardrobe of suits over his shoulder, as he departs Heathrow Airport for concerts in South America.
25th January, 1967

Facing page: Ballet dancer Rudolf Nureyev, who had defected from the Soviet Union in Paris six years previously, was well protected from the British winter weather when he left Heathrow Airport bound for Milan, Italy.
17th March, 1967

Goatee-bearded bandleader and clarinetist Acker Bilk, famous for his bowler hat and striped waistcoat, leaves Heathrow Airport for a concert tour in Germany.
8th March, 1967

Russian born Yul Brynner, the Hollywood actor whose deep, rich voice and smooth scalp became his trademark after his classic appearance in the 1956 film *The King and I*, boards an aircraft at Heathrow Airport.

23rd May, 1967

British actor Michael Caine on arrival at Heathrow Airport after filming in Spain, still resembling his character, the anti-hero secret agent Harry Palmer, in the soon to be released Ken Russell espionage thriller *Billion Dollar Brain*.
28th June, 1967

Facing page: Smiling comedian, television presenter and master ad-libber Bob Monkhouse shares a lighthearted moment with trendy dance troupe The Beat Girls at Gatwick Airport, where they were due to leave on tour.
28th July, 1967

Billie Jean King with her husband Larry before boarding an airliner at Heathrow Airport in London bound for New York. The American tennis player had just won a triple triumph: the Ladies Singles Final at Wimbledon, the Women's Doubles and the Mixed Doubles finals.
10th July, 1967

Welsh actor Richard Burton and his actress wife Elizabeth
Taylor at Heathrow Airport before departing for Sicily,
where they were to film the Franco Zeffirelli production of
Shakespeare's *The Taming of the Shrew*.
28th July, 1967

Identically outfitted and jumping for joy at Heathrow Airport are (L–R) Andrea Simpson and Lynne Gibson, The Caravelles singing duo, their stage name taken from the French airliner of the day.
15th August, 1967

Facing page: Twenty miniskirted British models pose at Heathrow Airport prior to their departure for Moscow. They are members of the British Clothing Export Council party, who are taking part in the Soviet Union's International Festival of Fashion to be held at the International Palace of Sports in the VI Lenin Stadium. It is expected that 120,000 Russians will watch the shows.
1st September, 1967

Eighteen year old model Twiggy, wearing black pantaloons with royal blue boots and a short fur jacket, at Heathrow Airport, where she left for Tokyo, Japan, to model and promote clothes made by her own fashion firm. Fourteen thousand seats were sold for her final Tokyo fashion show.
17th October, 1967

Facing page: Four British pop groups, bound for the United States on a tour that will yield 500,000 dollars, board their plane at Heathrow Airport. The groups are Jimi Hendrix Experience, Eric Burdon and the Animals, Alan Price Set and Éire Apparent. Hendrix's group was to receive a gold disc from Frank Sinatra's record company for their first LP *Are You Experienced?* passing the million dollar sales mark.

30th January, 1968

Shirley Bassey grins for the photographers as she leaves Heathrow Airport, in a black and white check coat trimmed with fur to match her fur hat. The singer was on her way to Beirut for a holiday.

11th December, 1967

Facing page: Gerry Anderson and his wife Sylvia seeing off puppets from their *Captain Scarlet and the Mysterons* television series, as they leave Heathrow Airport on a promotional visit to Japan. This was the first 'Supermarionation' offering from Century 21 Productions in which electronic improvements allowed miniaturisation of the lip-sync mechanisms so that the puppets could be built closer to human proportions than previous versions.
8th April, 1968

Johnny Cash, the American Country and Western singer, pictured with his wife of two months, singer-songwriter June Carter, at Heathrow Airport. Cash had proposed to her during a live performance in London, Ontario, Canada. Their love story was immortalised in the 2005 film *Walk The Line*.
2nd May, 1968

American film actor Marlon Brando, who had recently announced his decision to give up his film career and devote his time to working for the civil rights movement in the United States, on arrival at Heathrow Airport. He was to participate in a TV programme dealing with the US race problem.
14th May, 1968

Actress Zsa Zsa Gabor, in leopard skin coat and matching high boots, as she left Heathrow Airport for Budapest to visit her father's grave. Before leaving she said, dramatically: *"If you never see me again, you will know that I've been kept behind the Iron Curtain."*
4th October, 1968

Henry Cooper, the British and European heavyweight boxing champion, gets in a little extra exercise as he pushes trainer Victor Andretti along on the luggage trolley as they arrived at Heathrow Airport. They were leaving for Rome, where Cooper was to defend his European title.
10th March, 1969

German born American actress Marlene Dietrich and American actor, singer and comedian Danny Kaye (sporting an uncharacteristic beard) appear in happy mood on arrival at Heathrow Airport from New York.
21st March, 1969

Facing page: John Lennon holds Kyoko Cox, the six year old daughter of his Japanese wife, the artist and musician Yoko Ono, on the child's arrival at Heathrow Airport, where she had flown in from New York.
18th May, 1969

Flamboyant American pianist and showman Liberace, known for his extravagant stage outfits, in more restrained attire as he greets his mother Frances Liberace Casadonte at Heathrow Airport.
9th April, 1969

Facing page: British hairdresser Vidal Sassoon with his wife, American actress Beverley Adams and their one year old daughter Catya at London's Heathrow Airport.
3rd September, 1969

In sombre mood, French film star, Brigitte Bardot, accompanied by her German millionaire playboy husband, Gunther Sachs, from whom she was divorced a week prior to their arrival at Heathrow Airport from Paris.
7th October, 1969

Nancy Sinatra, 29 year old daughter of 'Ol' Blue Eyes' Frank, perched on the back of a BSA driven by record producer Mickey Most, who had met the singer at Heathrow Airport when she arrived to record *Highway Song* – making the motorcycle rather appropriate.
12th October, 1969

Apollo 11 astronauts (L–R) Neil Armstrong, Michael Collins and Edwin 'Buzz' Aldrin, with their wives Janet, Pat and Joan, touch down at Heathrow Airport during their 22-nation, 38 day world tour.
14th October, 1969

Fans mob rock 'n' roll
singer Gene Vincent for his
autograph on his arrival at
Heathrow Airport from Paris.
5th November, 1969

Goldie Hawn with her husband, film director Gus Trikonis, on arrival at Heathrow Airport from Paris. She was to attend the premiere of the science fiction film *Marooned*, starring Gregory Peck, at The Empire, Leicester Square, London.
29th January, 1970

A smiling British comedian and actor Peter Sellers takes the hand of his daughter Victoria at Heathrow Airport, while carrying her doll is her mother, the Swedish actress Britt Ekland, Sellers' former wife.
19th February, 1970

A game of cards relieves the tedium of waiting for a plane for members of the England party en route to Belgium from Heathrow Airport. (L–R) Geoff Hurst, Jeff Astle, Gordon Banks, Alan Ball, Tommy Wright and Jackie Charlton.

23rd February, 1970

Facing page: An Easter kiss for Duke D'Mond from his wife Pauline Palmer at Heathrow Airport. She was saying goodbye to him and his fellow Barron Knights, (L–R) Barron Anthony, Dave Ballinger, P'Nut Langford and Buth Baker at the start of their six week tour performing humorous pop parodies.
27th March, 1970

The England football squad at Heathrow Airport prior to leaving for Mexico and the World Cup tournament. Foreground is Jeff Astle playing a single on a portable record player as he waits with (L–R) Emlyn Hughes and Geoff Hurst for their departure. The England team were themselves hitting the top spot in the charts with their song *Back Home* released by Pye Records.
4th May, 1970

Facing page: England World Cup team manager, Sir Alf Ramsey (C in front of policeman), is surrounded by home supporters, who clamoured to meet the party on their return from Mexico, having lost the tournament 3-2 to Germany in the quarter finals.
17th June, 1970

Peggy Lee, international singing star, arrives at London's Heathrow Airport, to board her homeward-bound (Los Angeles) plane, after a triumphant solo concert at the Royal Concert Hall.
25th June, 1970

At an unhappy, troubled and drug-fuelled time of her life, the singer, songwriter and actress Marianne Faithfull arrives at Heathrow Airport, the month after she had ended her much publicised relationship with Rolling Stone Mick Jagger.
25th June, 1970

Facing page: English actress Joan Collins at Heathrow Airport with her future husband Ron Kass, the American businessman who had been president at Apple Records during the heyday of The Beatles.
7th August, 1970

Facing page: A rapturous welcome for English singer Engelbert Humperdinck as he returned to London from his American tour. He was to appear at the London Palladium for two weeks following a petition signed by 12,000 of his British fans imploring him to appear in the country again, after his phenomenal success in Las Vegas venues.
12th November, 1970

Mrs Jackie Onassis, wife of Greek shipping magnate Aristotle Onassis, and formerly the wife of John F Kennedy, President of the United States of America until his assassination in 1963, pictured at Heathrow Airport before flying to New York.
3rd January, 1971

Facing page: American actor Marlon Brando, with his hair drawn back into a ponytail, presents a picture of deep thought when arriving at Heathrow Airport. He was leaving for New York.
24 February, 1971

Soul singer James Brown with his wife Deirdre 'Deedee' Jenkins upon their arrival at Heathrow Airport.
9th March, 1971

Roy Orbison and his German wife Barbara are reunited at Heathrow Airport, with their seven month old son Roy Kelton. The couple had first met in the Batley Variety Club, Batley, West Yorkshire, a popular venue for stars such as Orbison.
21st April, 1971

Sporting a pair of sun-shaped shades and wearing blue denim, Scottish pop singer Lulu passes through Heathrow Airport with her husband Maurice Gibb of the Bee Gees.

21st April, 1971

Facing page: Former Beatle John Lennon at Heathrow Airport, who arrived with his wife Yoko Ono from New York on the eve of the second edition publication of Yoko's book *Grapefruit*, containing the artist's surreal, Zen-like instructions for art and life, originally published in 1964.
14th July, 1971

English-born French actress Jane Birkin with French songwriter Serge Gainsbourg at Heathrow Airport after arriving from Paris. After the furore of the pair's notorious release of *Je t'aime… moi non plus* in 1969, they had recorded Gainsburg's concept album *Histoire de Melody Nelson* in London.
22nd July, 1971

Welsh singer Tom Jones signs autographs for fans who
gathered at London's Heathrow Airport before he flew out to
Miami on the first leg of his five month American tour.
1st August, 1971

Bette Davis and Robert Wagner with his daughter Katherine at Heathrow Airport. The actors were leaving for Glasgow, Scotland to shoot the pilot for a new ABC television series, *Madame Sin*. Despite lavish sets and Bond style action, the film never made it to the network's schedule and was released as a feature film in 1972.

30th August, 1971

Facing page: Film director Alfred Hitchcock makes a telephone call at Heathrow Airport, before flying to Los Angeles, after completing the grisly thriller *Frenzy*.
23rd October, 1971

Pop singer Cilla Black carries her son across Heathrow's tarmac after flying in from Nice, France. Baby Robert would later become Cilla's manager, a role he inherited from his father Bobby Willis.
7th September, 1971

Motown singing group The Supremes at Heathrow Airport after arriving for a tour of Britain. (L–R) Jean Terrell, Cindy Birdsong and Mary Wilson.

9th November, 1971

American actress, singer and dancer Ann-Margret was pictured at Heathrow Airport wearing a man's style suit and trilby, with a red carnation buttonhole. Her husband Roger Smith, former star of TV detective series *77 Sunset Strip*, wore a similar suit and hat. They were travelling from Munich to Los Angeles, where she was to promote her film *Carnal Knowledge*.

28th January, 1972

Pop singer Olivia Newton-John leaves Heathrow Airport for a week's holiday in Los Angeles. A frequent guest on Cliff Richard's weekly TV show, she became the first female vocalist to perform duets with the singer, in a comedy film *The Case*.
12th February, 1972

Rudolf Nureyev, the ballet dancer, was well protected from the winter weather when he left Heathrow Airport wearing a fake fur cap, leather coat and knee-length boots, with a scarf round his neck. He was flying to Paris for a rehearsal, then on to Milan for a ballet appearance.

13th February, 1972

On his arrival back from the United States, Tom Jones, the Welsh pop singer, is besieged by fans. Most are delighted to have his autograph, but one young girl is seen excitedly hugging and kissing him.
21st March, 1972

Country singer Johnny Cash is pictured at Heathrow Airport carrying his son, John. Also with him is his wife, June Carter (L) and stepdaughter, Rosie (R).
24th September, 1972

English musician and aspiring politician Screaming Lord Sutch welcomes his bride-to-be – model Thann Rendessy from Chicago – by sweeping her off her feet at Heathrow Airport. The eccentric performer's reputation was founded on horror-themed stage shows with his band The Savages that predated other shock rock acts such as Alice Cooper.
10th January, 1973

British Glam Rock band The Sweet – (L–R) Mick Tucker,
Andy Scott, Steve Priest, and Brian Connolly – were enjoying
success as Top of the Pops in the UK with their single
Blockbuster when seen at Heathrow Airport about to leave
for a tour of the Far East.
13th February, 1973

Facing page: Sixteen year old teen idol Donny Osmond who, with his siblings Alan, Wayne, Merrill and Jay formed the successful Osmond Brothers singing group, is seen arriving at Heathrow Airport to be greeted by thousands of screaming fans. In addition to performing with his elder brothers, younger brother Jimmy and sister Marie, Donny had carved himself a solo career.
2nd March, 1973

American actress Mia Farrow with her recently adopted Vietnamese daughter Kym Lark, pictured at Heathrow Airport with her husband André Previn, the pianist, conductor and composer, before leaving for Boston, USA.
24th March, 1973

R&B and soul act from Atlanta, Georgia, USA, Gladys Knight and the Pips had been known for a string of hits, including *I Heard it Through the Grapevine* in 1967. The group, seen at Heathrow Airport, were very much a family affair, consisting of (L–R) William Guest, his cousin Gladys, another cousin Edward Patton, and Gladys' brother Merald 'Bubba' Knight.
10th May, 1973

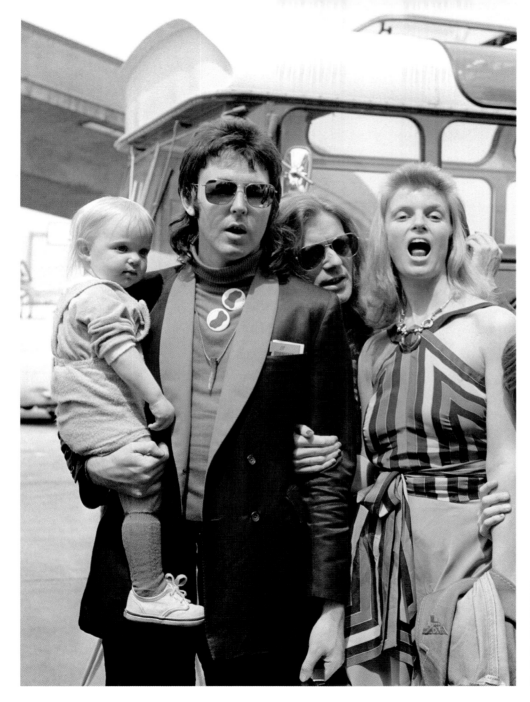

Former Beatles star Paul McCartney with his wife Linda and their daughter Stella at Heathrow Airport after flying from Glasgow with their group Wings.
25th May, 1973

Actress Diana Rigg and her husband of one week, artist Manachen Gueffen, at Heathrow Airport before leaving on a combined honeymoon and business trip to Los Angeles, USA.
15th July, 1973

American ballad singer Jack Jones, one of the most popular vocalists during the 1960s, highly regarded by Frank Sinatra and whom Judy Garland called 'the best jazz singer in the world', arrives at Heathrow Airport from the US. The singer has a strong following in Britain, which he visits most years.

21st September, 1973

A photo opportunity for star
Manchester United footballer
George Best (L) and the
team's manager Tommy
Docherty at Heathrow
Airport before they left for
Lisbon, in Portugal.
24th September, 1973

Charismatic American actor
James Coburn and his wife
Beverly Kelly on arrival at
Heathrow Airport from
Los Angeles.
16th October, 1973

Back from a five month tour of America, The New Seekers:
(L–R) Marty Kristian, Eve Graham, new member Peter Oliver,
Lyn Paul and Paul Layton. Peter Oliver joined the group to
replace Peter Doyle, whose decision to leave the group had
shocked fans earlier in the year.
16th October, 1973

Actor-singer David Essex
with his wife Maureen and
their two year old daughter
Verity at Heathrow Airport.
5th January, 1974

Greek singer Demis Roussos leaves Heathrow Airport for a tour of Scandinavia. Once part of the progressive rock band Aphrodite's Child, along with fellow Greek Vangelis, Roussos was enjoying solo success with chart-topping songs such as *Forever and Ever*.

10th April, 1974

Facing page: American singer 'Mama' Cass Elliott arrives at Heathrow Airport, accompanied by Mervyn Laird (L) and Walter Painter, a choreographer.

10th May, 1974

Facing page: The 'Daddy of Rock', American singer Bill Haley and his wife Martha. The couple flew in to Heathrow from Brussels, Belgium, en route for Los Angeles, USA, clutching a replica of the famous fountain, *Manneken Pis*.
15th May, 1974

David Cassidy, American actor and singer, from *The Partridge Family* musical sitcom, enjoying a solo pop career in the 1970s, arrives at Heathrow Airport for the last dates in his world concert tour. On the penultimate show, four days after this photograph was taken, a gate stampede at London's White City Stadium injured 650 in a crush at the front of the stage, and a 14 year old girl later died.
22nd May, 1974

The Bee Gees (L–R) Barry, Maurice and Robin Gibb at Heathrow Airport before leaving for a three month world tour.
20th August, 1974

Ex-Beatle Ringo Starr at Heathrow airport before a flight to Los Angeles, USA. Starr remarked that he was no longer interested in performing live.
8th November, 1974

Facing page: Steve Harley (C) flanked by members of his band Cockney Rebel, were top of the pop charts with *Make me Smile (Come Up and See Me)*, when they arrived at Heathrow Airport fresh from a two-week tour of one-night stands in the USA.

26th February, 1975

Ever the clown, Welsh entertainer Harry Secombe flamboyantly stretches out his arms in order to be security searched at Heathrow Airport.

1st February, 1975

Influential American rock 'n' roll singer and guitarist Chuck Berry arrives at Heathrow Airport. The musician toured for much of the 1970s, often carrying only his Gibson guitar, and hiring backing bands as he went, so confident was he in his music and fame.

7th March, 1975

Shaven headed *Kojak* actor
Telly Savalas at Heathrow
Airport after arriving from
Los Angeles, USA en route
for South Africa where he
was to star in the thriller
Killer Force, about diamond
smuggling, with Peter Fonda.
3rd May, 1975

Facing page: Doo wop and R&B vocal group The Drifters, on arrival at Heathrow Airport for their four week tour, comprise (L–R) Grant Kitching, Butch Leak, Clyde Brown and Johnny Moore.
17th July, 1975

British singer Englebert Humperdink arriving at Heathrow Airport fresh from a successful American tour.
24th September, 1975

The Bay City Rollers pop group (L–R) Stuart 'Woody' Wood, Alan Longmuir, Leslie McKeown, Derek Longmuir, and Eric Faulkner on board a jumbo jet at Heathrow Airport before leaving for Perth and a tour of Australia.
26th November, 1975

American actress and singer Eartha Kitt, at Heathrow Airport, when she left for home in Los Angeles after completing a gruelling world tour.
8th December, 1975

Singer Diana Ross, shouldering a rather large music machine complete with earphones – a far cry from the iPods of today – on arrival at Heathrow for her tour of Britain.
9th March, 1976

Debonair actor David Niven at Heathrow Airport, where he was leaving to greet his son on a three-day visit in New York.
8th April, 1976

Voluptuous American singer Dolly Parton arrived at
Heathrow Airport to take part in the eighth International
Festival of Country Music at Wembley.
16th April, 1976

Bizarre international travelling attire from American rock band
Kiss (L–R) Paul Stanley, Gene Simmons, Ace Frehley and Peter
Criss, as they arrived at Heathrow Airport for their British tour.
10th May, 1976

Facing page: Keith Moon, wildman drummer with the The Who, at Heathrow, takes the wheel of an airport luggage transporter. He was flying in from Los Angeles to join the other members of the group for a tour of England and France.
16th May, 1976

American pop group The Three Degrees (L–R) Sheila Ferguson, Fayette Pinkney and Valerie Holiday at Heathrow Airport.
13th May, 1976

Facing page: Rod Stewart, dressed dramatically in a cloak and dark glasses, and his actress girlfriend Britt Ekland make their way through Heathrow Airport on their way to Paris.
18th May, 1976

American actor Robert Wagner and his actress wife Natalie Wood at a stop off at Heathrow Airport before leaving to present the awards at the Cannes Film Festival, France.
28th May, 1976

Eight year old Patsy Kensit before leaving Heathrow Airport for Moscow, USSR to attend the premiere of her new film *The Blue Bird of Happiness,* in which she plays alongside Elizabeth Taylor as her screen daughter, Mytyl in George Cukor's Soviet-American production.
9th June, 1976

American actor Telly Savalas – popular television detective Theo Kojak – takes a break at Heathrow Airport, where he was due to leave for Los Angeles, USA.
16th June, 1976

Facing page: Swedish pop group ABBA (L–R) Benny Andersson, Anni-Frid Lyngstad, Agnetha Fältskog and Björn Ulvaeus at Heathrow Airport. The previous week Anni-Frid had released her solo album, which featured a Swedish version of the song *Fernando*, written by Ulvaeus, Andersson, and the band's manager Stig Anderson. So successful was the song that it was re-recorded in English and became one of ABBA's best-selling singles, topping the charts in thirteen countries.
15th November, 1976

Elton John in red and blue Wellington boots as he left Heathrow Airport for a two-day business trip to America. The boots, which Elton said should be described as 'after ski-boots', were just part of a zany outfit comprising a green and pink jacket, blue tracksuit bottoms and a black and gold scarf.
9th January, 1977

Relaxed and beaming, film star Cary Grant paused for cameras at London's Heathrow Airport returning to Los Angeles, USA after a business trip to Britain.
22nd February, 1977

Perched on the front bumper of a classic Rolls Royce, the Victoria Sporting Club's New Award for Talent was presented to Sammy Davis Jr by Georgina Warwick on his arrival at Heathrow Airport, for a holiday in Britain.

25th February, 1977

Singer Jerry Lee Lewis as he left Heathrow for Paris. The singer had been involved in an altercation after reporters questioned him about the criticism of his concerts in the press.
28th February, 1977

Phil Bennett, the British Lions rugby union team captain, holding the team's mascot at Heathrow Airport, before they left for their 25-match tour of New Zealand.
10th May, 1977

Facing page: Former Page Three models (L–R) Jilly Johnson and Nina Carter at Heathrow Airport where, as the singing duo Blonde on Blonde they were on their way to Glasgow to promote their debut single *Subway*.
18th July, 1977

Prince Andrew, 17, carries his own suitcase at Heathrow Airport, on his return from Canada where he has been studying at Lakefield College School in Ontario for six months under an exchange scheme with Gordonstoun school.
4th June, 1977

Detroit-born singer-songwriter Suzi Quatro, who moved to the UK in 1971 after being discovered by Mickie Most, is seen at Heathrow Airport before flying off to Los Angeles, USA to appear on American Television. Quatro played the role of Leather Tuscadero, fronting an all-girl rock band, in the TV show *Happy Days*.
12th August, 1977

Leo Sayer and his wife Janice on arrival at Heathrow Airport from his successful 52-date tour of North America. The artist, who had started his singing career wearing a pierrot style outfit and clown's makeup, enjoyed a string of hits, including a 1976 Number 1 in the USA, with *You Make Me Feel Like Dancing*.
14th September, 1977

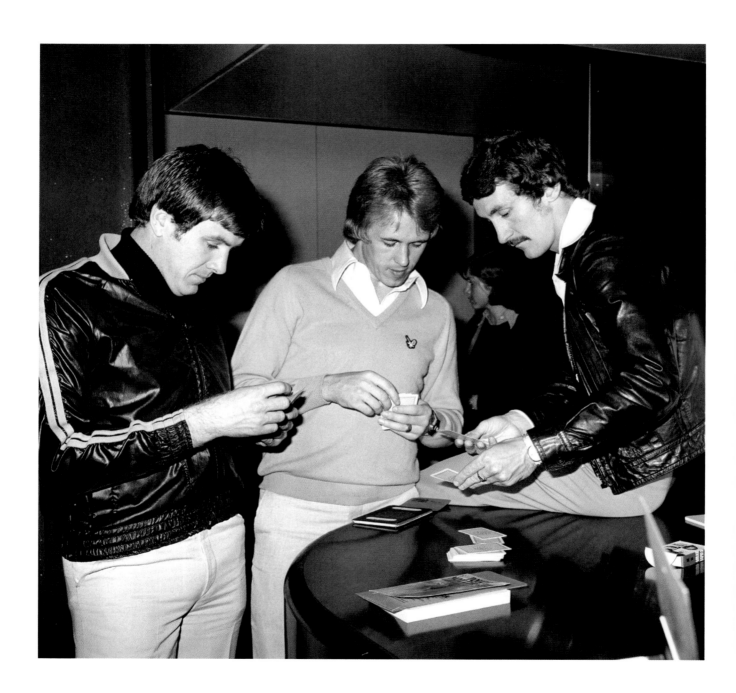

Facing page: England football players (L–R) captain Emlyn Hughes and his Liverpool team mates Phil Neal and Terry McDermott, enjoy a game of cards at Heathrow Airport before flying with the squad for their World Cup qualifier against Luxembourg.
10th October, 1977

American disco music singer Donna Summer arrives at Heathrow Airport for her sold out concert tour of Britain.
21st October, 1977

Bassist Sid Vicious (L) and lead vocalist Johnny Rotten, members of the controversial punk rock group The Sex Pistols, at Heathrow Airport before leaving for Luxembourg. In typical anarchic fashion they hurled abuse at reporters and photographers as they walked to their aircraft.
3rd November, 1977

Texan country music singing star Kenny Rogers at Heathrow Airport when he arrived with his two favourite ladies – his bride of a few weeks, television star Marianne Gordon (L) and the lovely Crystal Gayle (R) who was joining him on his British tour.

4th November, 1977

Facing page: The Queen arriving at Heathrow Central station in the driver's cab of a tube train, when she officially opened the £30 million Piccadilly Line extension linking Heathrow Airport with London's underground railway system.
16th December, 1977

Barely recognisable in fur hat and sunglasses, singer Cher was pictured at Heathrow Airport with her children Chastity, 8, her daughter from her marriage to Sonny Bono, and 18 month old son Elijah Blue from her second marriage to singer Gregg Allman.
27th November, 1977

Pop superstars (L–R) Rod
Stewart and Elton John,
who was wearing contact
lenses instead of his usual
flamboyant glasses, at
Heathrow Airport when they
flew in after holidaying in
Rio de Janeiro.

8th February, 1978

Anni-Frid Lyngstad and Benny Andersson, from chart topping ABBA, at Heathrow Airport as they arrive for the premiere of their film *Abba: The Movie*. The couple had been engaged for several years, and married in October 1978, only to divorce in 1981 after problems arose during the height of the band's success.

14th February, 1978

Influential singer-songwriter
Bob Dylan arrives at
Heathrow Airport, for a
sell-out concert at London's
Earls Court.
12th June, 1978

British World Champion Grand Prix motorcyclist Barry Sheene at Heathrow Airport with girlfriend Stephanie McClean before flying to Helsinki. Former *Penthouse* model Miss McClean had met Sheene when he was on crutches following a racing accident.
27th July, 1978

Singer-songwriter Barry Manilow, a superstar back home in the United States, where five of his albums were on the best-selling charts simultaneously, arrived at Heathrow Airport from Chicago at the start of a British tour.
2nd October, 1978

Facing page: Malcolm McLaren, manager of punk group the Sex Pistols, at Heathrow Airport prior to flying to New York, where group member Sid Vicious was to appear in court accused of knifing to death his girlfriend Nancy Spungen on the 12th of October.
13th October, 1978

West Germany-based pop and disco group Boney M, (L–R)
Liz Mitchell, Mazie Williams, Bobby Farrell and Marcia Barrett,
arriving at Heathrow Airport after their successful Russian tour.
The group gave ten sell-out concerts in Moscow but, by special
request of the authorities, did not include their hit *Rasputin
(Russia's Greatest Love Machine)*.
14th December, 1978

Michael Jackson (C) with his brothers (L–R) Marlon, Jackie, Randy and Tito make up The Jackson 5, one of the biggest pop music phenomena of the 1970s, seen arriving at Heathrow Airport from Amsterdam for their British tour.
4th February, 1979

Facing page: American soul singer Gladys Knight at Heathrow Airport when she arrived from Los Angeles for a British concert tour.
10th October, 1979

American actor Walter Matthau at Heathrow Airport, where he left for Los Angeles to finish filming *Hopscotch*, a comedy in which he played Miles Kendig, a renegade CIA agent, alongside British actress Glenda Jackson.
7th November, 1979

The Police at Heathrow Airport (L–R), Andy Summers, Sting and Stewart Copeland, bound for Ireland. The group were to take to the stage at Croke Park as part of their global reunion tour. Some 82,000 tickets went on sale for the Dublin concert in April the previous year, all of which were snapped up within hours.
19th January, 1980

British rock band The Tourists, at Heathrow Airport: (L–R) Annie Lennox, Peet Coombes, Jim 'Do It' Toomey and Eddie Chin. Missing is guitarist Dave Stewart who, with Coombes, formed the nucleus of the band. Stewart and Lennox's relationship, and the band, broke up during this year, although the pair went on to form the highly successful Eurythmics.
11th March, 1980

Actor-singer David Soul, who found fame with British TV viewers playing Hutch in the American police series *Starsky and Hutch*, at Heathrow Airport when he left for Los Angeles after a nationwide singing tour.

3rd April, 1980

Two members of the British twelve-bar-blues band Status Quo, (L–R) Francis Rossi and Rick Parfitt, on arrival at Heathrow Airport.
19th May, 1980

Facing page: Rod Stewart, his wife Alana Hamilton, and baby Kimberly aged 10 months at Heathrow Airport, where they were to join a Concorde flight for New York.
14th June, 1980

Motown recording star, Marvin Gaye, holding his happy looking four year old son Frankie, on their arrival at Heathrow Airport from San Francisco, USA. Marvin is to undertake a British and European concert tour starting at London's Royal Albert Hall.
12th June, 1980

Veteran film actor Jim Davis, who plays Texas oil tycoon Jock Ewing in *Dallas*, the American prime-time television soap opera, and his wife Blanche at Heathrow Airport.
22nd September, 1980

Effervescent British pop group Bucks Fizz at Heathrow Airport, returning with their trophy on winning the Eurovision Song Contest in Dublin, Ireland with their song *Making Your Mind Up*, (L–R): Michael Nolan, Cheryl Baker, Jay Aston and Bobby G.
5th April, 1981

Facing page: Diana, Princess of Wales, waves goodbye at the door of an RAF Andover turbo-prop aircraft at Eastleigh Airport, Southampton, before departing for her honeymoon with Prince Charles, seen behind her.
1st August, 1981

American entertainer Sammy Davies Junior, and his wife, Altovise, at Heathrow Airport after arriving from New York. He is to perform eight London concerts, including a charity show in aid of Tel Aviv university.
19th June, 1981

Facing page: Corgi puppies being carried on to an Andover aircraft, as the Queen arrives at Heathrow Airport to connect with a flight to Aberdeen, Scotland and the start of her annual holiday at Balmoral.
5th August, 1981

England cricketer Ian Botham seated in the cockpit of a Cessna 152 after taking a lesson in his private pilot's license course.
21st August, 1981

Rocky star Sylvester Stallone arrives at Heathrow Airport to attend the gala charity premiere of his latest movie *Escape to Victory,* in which he stars alongside Michael Caine, at the Odeon cinema in Leicester Square, London.
1st September, 1981

Stuart Goddard, better known to his fans as Adam of new wave band Adam and the Ants, at Heathrow Airport when the group left for New York at the start of their world tour. Behind can be seen his girlfriend, actress Amanda Donohoe, who appeared in the video for the Ants' most successful single *Stand And Deliver*.

6th September, 1981

Facing page: Gay campaigner, writer and raconteur Quentin Crisp, whose memoir, *The Naked Civil Servant*, was the subject of a television film starring John Hurt, is seen at Heathrow Airport before flying to New York, where he was to live.
September, 1981

English broadcaster and journalist Michael Parkinson, affectionately known as 'Parky', and his wife Mary presented a picture of togetherness at Heathrow Airport, when they arrived on a flight from Australia.
7th September, 1981

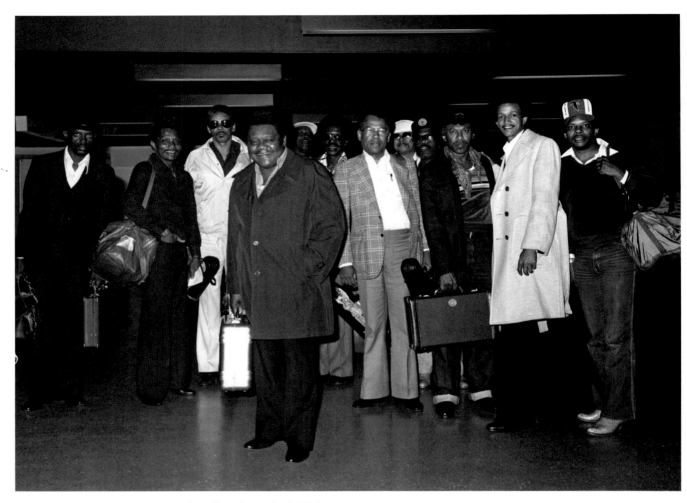

American jazz pianist Fats
Domino (foreground) and
members of his band pause
for a group photograph after
jetting into Heathrow Airport
from the United States.
18th October, 1981

Sporting a checked coat and hat, actor Peter O'Toole makes his way to the departure gate at Heathrow Airport prior to flying to New York by Concorde.

11th January, 1982

American actress Faye Dunaway and her boyfriend, fashion and celebrity photographer Terry O'Neill glimpsed at Heathrow Airport, prior to flying out to New York. O'Neill's career took off in 1959 when, a trainee in BOAC's technical photographic unit at Heathrow, he snapped the sleeping figure of the British Home Secretary Rab Butler, which became a front page newspaper image the following day.
15th May, 1982

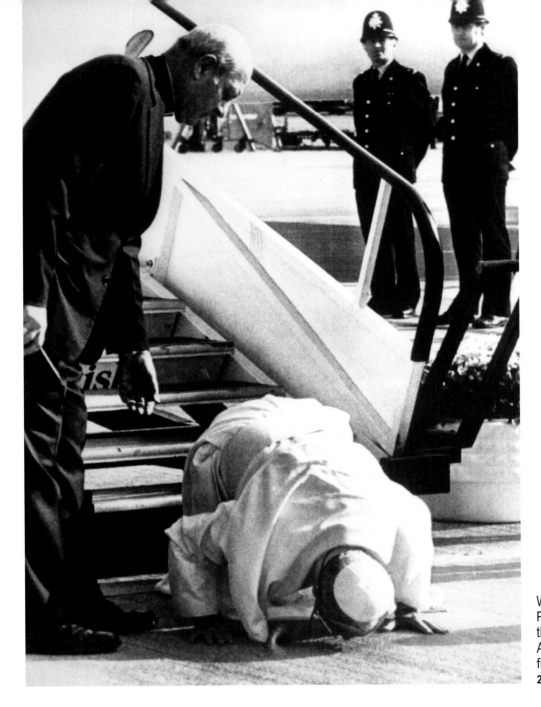

Watched by an aide,
Pope John Paul II kisses
the tarmac at Gatwick
Airport upon alighting
from his plane.
29th May, 1982

Arriving in London for the world premiere of the film *Gandhi* are (L–R) Sir Richard Attenborough, director; Ben Kingsley, who plays the Indian statesman; and Sir John Mills, who plays the Viceroy.

1st December, 1982

Eric Clapton and his wife, model and photographer Pattie Boyd in Heathrow Airport, as they leave for Los Angeles. The former wife of George Harrison of the Beatles, Miss Boyd was the inspiration for love songs written by both men, notably Harrison's *Something*, and Clapton's *Wonderful Tonight*.
10th January, 1983

Facing page: Arriving at Heathrow Airport are (L–R) film director Stephen Spielberg, actor Harrison Ford and actress Kate Capshaw: the three were en route during production of *Indiana Jones and the Temple of Doom*, second of the blockbusting adventure movies starring Ford in the title role. Miss Capshaw plays Wilhelmina 'Willie' Scott, love interest for 'Indy' while, in reality, Spielberg and Capshaw were to form a relationship during casting and subsequently married.
14th March, 1983

Pop singer Boy George, complete with characteristic dreadlocks and kaftan leaves Heathrow Airport for a promotional trip to the United States, along with Culture Club band member Roy Hay (L).
28th June, 1983

Facing page: Eric Clapton and Phil Collins at Heathrow Airport leaving for Antigua where they are to work on a new album together.
6th March, 1984

Michael Caine and his wife, the model and actress Shakira at Heathrow Airport. The couple had been married since 1973. Caine had seen his future wife in a television Maxwell House coffee advert, and a friend gave him her telephone number. The rest is history, and they are together to this day.
12th February, 1984

That much travelled jetsetter Daisy with her parents Scottish comedian Billy Connolly and New Zealand comedian and actress Pamela Stephenson, leaving Heathrow Airport, for Los Angeles. Billy had just finished filming *Water* with Michael Caine in the West Country.
14th August, 1984

British athlete Sebastian Coe proudly displays his gold and silver medals when he arrived at Heathrow Airport from the Los Angeles Olympic Games. Coe won the 1500 metres and came second in the 800 metres.
14th August, 1984

Actress Sophia Loren and party at Heathrow Airport between her incoming flight from Geneva and her flight to Los Angeles.
12th September, 1984

A young fan in the making, 11 month old Michael Voss of Hounslow crawled to a sitting position at the feet of comedian and actor Dudley Moore with his girlfriend Susan Anton at Heathrow Airport, stopping them in their tracks, before the American singer could board her plane.

16th October, 1984

Recoiling from the flash of press cameras, comedian Jasper Carrott, 39, at Heathrow Airport when he returned from Los Angeles where he rounded off his two month tour of the United States.

14th November, 1984

Facing page: Prime Minister Margaret Thatcher sitting in the cockpit of her Royal Air Force VC-10 during a flight to Hong Kong from Peking.

20th December, 1984

Dressed in an Arabic *thobe*, headcloth and rope circlet, David Essex arrived at Heathrow Airport, after a visit to Dubai, where the singer had been on an eight-performance tour of the Middle East.
20th December, 1984

Facing page: Andrew Ridgeley (L) and George Michael of the pop duo Wham! at Heathrow Airport before leaving for a tour of Japan.
5th January, 1985

Child actor and later
Spandau Ballet bassist
Martin Kemp drapes an arm
over the shoulder of girlfriend
Shirlie Holliman at Heathrow
Airport, after flying in from
New York. Kemp played with
his brother Gary in the New
Romantic band, and met his
future wife when she was a
backing singer for Wham!
11th May, 1985

American actor Patrick Duffy, who plays Bobby Ewing in the television soap series *Dallas*, arriving at Heathrow Airport from Los Angeles to make a promotional video.

13th May, 1985

Actress and singer Cher, 40, fresh from the Cannes Film Festival where she won a joint Best Actress award for her hit film *Mask*, at Heathrow Airport, prior to flying to New York.
24th May, 1985

DJ and entertainer Kenny Everett (R) at London's Heathrow Airport accompanied by a friend whose name he would reveal only as Brian, when he left for a holiday in Madrid.
1st January, 1986

The newly-wed Duke and Duchess of York wave to watching well-wishers as they board a jet at Heathrow Airport, which would carry them to the Azores for their honeymoon.
23rd July, 1986

Virgin boss Richard Branson with his friend, the Swedish balloon pilot and adventurer Per Lindstrand at Gatwick Airport, to see off the final cargo of equipment for their upcoming challenge in which they will attempt to cross the Atlantic in a hot-air balloon.

16th June, 1987

Blonde American singer and actress Madonna arrives at
Leeds Bradford International Airport, on the way to her first
British concert at Roundhay Park, in Leeds.
15th August, 1987

Fans eagerly await the
arrival of Madonna at
Heathrow Airport.
16th August, 1987

The triumphant European golf team pose with the Ryder Cup
at Heathrow Airport on their return to England: (back L–R)
José Rivero, Gordon Brand Jr, Sam Torrance, Ian Woosnam;
(centre L–R) Eamonn Darcy, Howard Clark, José María
Olazábal (hidden), Bernhard Langer, Nick Faldo; (front, L–R)
Severiano Ballesteros, captain Tony Jacklin.
28th September, 1987

British actress Joan Collins, queen of the soap stars, lives up to her glamorous image on arrival at Heathrow from Los Angeles, wearing an all white outfit with glittering gold buckle.

21st January, 1988

A *'howdy folks'* greeting from Cheltenham's ski-jump hero of the Winter Olympics, Eddie 'The Eagle' Edwards, on arrival at Heathrow from Calgary with the rest of the team. Plasterer Edwards had been the sole British applicant for the competition, and was totally self-funded. Using borrowed equipment short-sighted Edwards battled in the face of adversity, winning worldwide affection for his efforts despite coming last in both the 70m and 90m events.
1st March, 1988

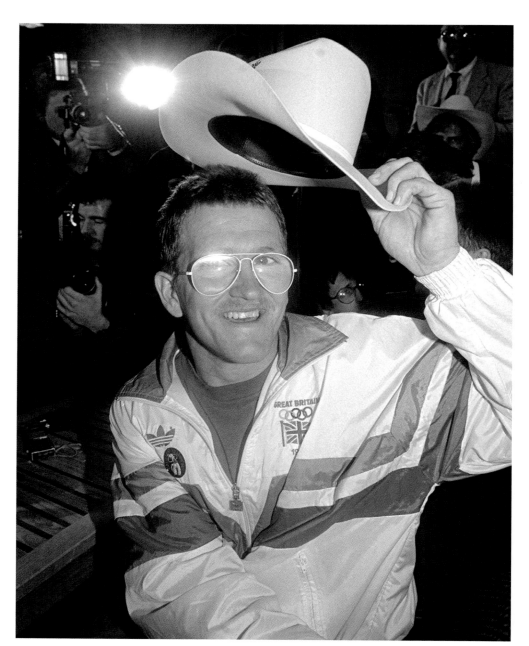

Michael Jackson fans await the arrival of the pop superstar
on the roof of the Queen's Building at Heathrow Airport.
Jackson was due to kick off the British leg of his world tour
with a concert at Wembley Stadium on the 14th of July.
11th July, 1988

Actress and pop singer Kylie Minogue and actor Jason Donovan, stars of *Neighbours*, one of Britain's favourite Australian TV soap operas, at Heathrow Airport after flying in from Sydney.
9th April, 1989

Twin brothers Matt and Luke
Goss of the pop duo Bros
pose with police at Heathrow
Airport before their flight to
Los Angeles for the start of
their American tour.
21st August, 1989

Four of the five members of American pop group New Kids on the Block arriving at Heathrow Airport from Vienna: (L–R) Jon Knight, Joey McIntyre, Donnie Wahlberg and Jordan Knight.
1st December, 1991

American actor Christopher Reeve, who played Superman in the groundbreaking movie of the same name, with his two children Matthew and Alexandra at Heathrow Airport, leaving to spend Christmas in New York.
15th December, 1991

Actor Anthony Hopkins holds the Academy Award he received for his role as the terrifying Hannibal Lecter, in the film *The Silence of the Lambs*, as he arrives at Heathrow Airport with his wife Jenny.
2nd April, 1992

American pop singer
Madonna at Heathrow
Airport before boarding her
Concorde flight to New York.
13th October, 1992

Oasis singer Liam Gallagher
checks in for his British
Airways flight to Chicago at
Heathrow Airport.
29th August, 1996

Racing driver Damon Hill
with his wife Georgie are
greeted at Heathrow Airport
when he arrived back in
Britain from Japan after
taking the Formula One
World Championship.
15th October, 1996

Former *Baywatch* star Pamela Anderson arrives at Heathrow Airport without baby Brandon or husband Tommy Lee. The star is heading for London to hold top level talks with Pizza Hut directors about making a comic advert for the restaurant.
4th February, 1997

Labour leader Tony Blair
during a flight from London
to Scotland on the final day
of campaigning before the
general election.
30th April, 1997

Arnold Schwarzenegger and wife Maria at Luton Airport, after
flying in on a specially painted 'Batplane' on the eve of the
London premiere of *Batman & Robin*, with George Clooney and
Chris O'Donnell in the title roles. The movie was the big budget
sequel to 1995's *Batman Forever*, and the 'Dynamic Duo' was
up against Arnie in the role of villain Mr Freeze.
22nd June, 1997

Hillary Clinton, the wife of
American President Bill
Clinton, arrives at Heathrow
Airport for the funeral of
Diana, Princess of Wales.
6th September, 1997

Superstar actress Joan Collins (R) teams up with *Coronation Street's* Jack (Bill Tarmey) and Vera Duckworth (Liz Dawn) in the soap's Christmas video. Miss Collins, 64, makes a cameo appearance when Jack and Vera fly home from Las Vegas to London's Heathrow Airport.

1st October, 1997

Comics and co-presenters of BBC 1's *Fantasy Football League* (L–R) Frank Skinner and David Baddiel kiss the tarmac of Rome's Ciampino Airport after arriving on an especially liveried jet before watching England's successful 0-0 World Cup qualifying draw against Italy, ensuring entry in the 1998 finals in Rome.

12th October, 1997

England midfielders David Beckham (front) and Darren Anderton disembark from their plane at Heathrow Airport following the England squad's return from the 1998 World Cup in France, where they were knocked out in the second-round by Argentina 4-3 in a penalty shoot-out.
1st July, 1998

American pop star Britney Spears arrives at Dublin Airport, for the MTV Europe Music Awards, which were to take place at The Point in Dublin on the 11th of November.

9th November, 1999

Hollywood actor Michael Douglas, nominated as a United Nations ambassador on nuclear disarmament, arrives at Heathrow Airport from Los Angeles, to urge British MPs to persuade the USA and Russia to reduce stockpiles of nuclear weapons.

20th March, 2000

Hollywood actress Elizabeth Taylor arrives at Heathrow from Los Angeles, to be made a Dame by the Queen. The 68 year old British-born actress said she was thrilled to be receiving the honour, declaring: *"It's the peak of my life"*. The eight-times married star, who wed Welsh-born actor Richard Burton twice, vowed she would never tie the knot again when asked if there was currently a man in her life.

13th May, 2000

Boxer Mike Tyson arrives at Heathrow Airport. He was to prepare for his controversial fight the following weekend against fellow American Lou Savarese at Hampden Park in Glasgow. The 33 year old had been due to fly to London several days previously but delayed his arrival to attend the funeral of a close friend who was shot dead in the Bronx area of New York, USA.

18th June, 2000

Actor Neil Morrissey is presented with a glass of champagne to celebrate his alter ego Bob the Builder's second Number 1 single: his version of Lou Bega's *Mamba Number 5*. Morrissey is travelling to Canada for the Toronto film festival.
9th September, 2001

Facing page: Palestinian leader Yasser Arafat arrives at Heathrow Airport. During his visit, made at the invitation of Prime Minister Tony Blair, Arafat was to discuss the international terror crisis and the implications of Allied air strikes on Afghanistan for the wider Middle East. Blair and Arafat were also expected to talk about how the Middle East peace process could be reinvigorated.
14th October, 2001

Irish pop singer Ronan Keating at Gatwick Airport heading for a Virgin Atlantic flight to Toronto.
9th September, 2001

Actress Kate Winslet
with her baby Mia leaves
Heathrow Airport for
Los Angeles.
26th February, 2002

Yoko Ono, the widow of former Beatle John Lennon, unveils a statue of her late husband on the upper concourse of Liverpool's John Lennon Airport. She was joined at the unveiling by Cherie Booth, wife of UK Prime Minister Tony Blair. The statue is the work of sculptor Tom Murphy.
15th March, 2002

American actor John Travolta – a qualified airline pilot – waves the Union Flag from the cockpit of his own 707 jet during a photocall at Heathrow Airport, as part of his 13-city Spirit of Friendship tour as the official Qantas 'Ambassador-at-Large'.
19th August, 2002

Sir Bob Geldof arrives at Heathrow Airport from starvation-hit Ethiopia, having blasted the European Union, world leaders and even Band Aid's hit song during the visit. The Irish former rock star had been visiting areas of the country affected by drought, describing failure to provide aid as *"criminal negligence"*.
3rd June, 2003

REM's lead singer Michael Stipe at Edinburgh Airport, after appearing at the MTV Europe Music Awards in Edinburgh.
7th November, 2003

Facing page: Contestant in *I'm a Celebrity...Get Me out of Here!* the reality TV series in which celebrities live in jungle conditions, glamour model Jordan arrives back from Australia at Heathrow Airport. During the show she famously fell out with John Lydon (formerly Johnny Rotten of the Sex Pistols), and flirted with singer Peter André, who she later married.
12th February, 2004

Gold medalists Matthew Pinsent and Kelly Holmes with
Silver medalist Amir Khan showing off their medals after a
news conference at Gatwick Airport, after TeamGB arrived
home from the Athens Olympic Games with nine Gold, nine
Silver and 12 Bronze medals.
30th August, 2004

Model Jodie Kidd on the wing of a Hawker 125 jet as she became the first club member of Club 328, at Southampton Airport before the official launch of the Club in Monaco.
21st September, 2004

I'm a Celebrity...Get Me out of Here! contestants Nancy Sorrell and her husband Jim Moir, otherwise known as the comedian Vic Reeves, arrive back at Heathrow Airport after their stint in the Australian jungle reality show.
9th December, 2004

Prime Minister Tony Blair signs the side of a British Airways 747 aircraft, which will become a flying petition with signatures of celebrities, passengers and staff to support London's bid for the 2012 Olympics.
27th April, 2005

Facing page: The Dalai Lama arrives at Edinburgh Airport from the USA, before he later plans to address an event aiming to give Tibet a more stable future. The exiled Buddhist leader will speak at the fourth World Parliamentarians Convention on Tibet in Edinburgh, during a two-day visit to the Scottish capital.
18th November, 2005

James Brown arriving at Edinburgh Airport, on the eve of the Live 8 concert to be held at Murrayfield Stadium. Coinciding with the 20th anniversary of Live Aid, the Live 8 concerts were a series of benefits in G8 states and in South Africa, timed to precede the G8 Conference and Summit to be held at the Gleneagles Hotel, Auchterarder, Scotland from the 6-8th of July.
5th July, 2005

Brad Pitt and Angelina Jolie at Heathrow Airport, where
they are due to leave the UK on a flight to Zurich. The pair
had starred in the 2005 film *Mr & Mrs Smith*, the tale of a
bored married couple, who discover that they are both secret
assassins. Their onscreen chemistry was much discussed in
the media.
25th January, 2006

England football coach Sven Goran Eriksson and his partner Nancy Dell'Olio at Stansted Airport in Essex, as the team return from Germany after they were knocked out of the World Cup quarter finals by Portugal.
2nd July, 2006

English indie band Babyshambles' lead singer Pete Doherty and supermodel girlfriend Kate Moss arrive at Dublin Airport for a Babyshambles gig in Carlow. Well publicised drug use has led to convictions and jail time for the troubled musician.
25th September, 2006

Four original members of the boy band Take That, (L–R) Gary Barlow, Howard Donald, Mark Owen and Jason Orange, pose at RAF Northolt Airport on the stairs of a private jet that will ferry the band between CD signings in London and Manchester. Since their Reunion Tour earlier in the year they had launched their first album in over ten years, *Beautiful World*, to critical acclaim.

27th November, 2006

Dame Helen Mirren arrives back at Heathrow Airport, after winning Best Actress at the Oscars for her role in *The Queen*.
27th February, 2007

Brazilian football player
Ronaldinho signs autographs
for fans after arriving at
Heathrow Airport. Brazil were
to play England in a Friendly
International at Wembley
Stadium on the 1st of June.
30th May, 2007

David Beckham arrives back at Heathrow Airport after his father Ted suffered a heart attack. The former England captain boarded a flight in Los Angeles the previous evening, on hearing the news that his father had been taken ill.
27th September, 2007

Members of the Spice Girls, (L–R) Victoria, Geri, Mel B, Emma and Mel C, open Virgin Atlantic's New Terminal at Heathrow Airport with Sir Richard Branson. The girls helped Branson open the check in as part of the redevelopment of Terminal 3 at the airport.

13th December, 2007

American socialite, heiress, model and singer Paris Hilton and Benji Madden, guitarist with Good Charlotte, walk around Airside departures of Terminal 1 at Heathrow Airport. The celebutante had announced her intention to marry tattooed Madden, a short lived engagement.
19th March, 2008

French President Sarkozy and wife Carla Bruni are met by
the Prince of Wales and the Duchess of Cornwall as they
arrive at Heathrow Airport. President Nicolas Sarkozy called
for closer ties between France and Britain as he kicked off
his first state visit to this country.
26th March, 2008

GORDON RAMSAY

PLANE FOOD

Characteristically irascible celebrity chef Gordon Ramsay launches his new restaurant, Plane Food, in Heathrow's new Terminal 5. The £4.3bn Terminal 5 (T5) opened for business on the same day, with the first plane landing eight minutes early.
27th March, 2008

Manchester United manager Sir Alex Ferguson arrives with the UEFA Champions League Trophy at Manchester Airport. Manchester United won the Champions League final in Moscow the previous night, beating Chelsea 6-5 on penalties after the match finished 1-1 following extra time.

22nd May, 2008

American President George W Bush and his wife Laura prepare to leave Heathrow Airport, as part of the president's 'farewell tour' of Europe. Mr Bush had been visiting France, Germany and Italy and was due to attend meetings with Prime Minister Gordon Brown and former premier Tony Blair, and to take tea with the Queen. The Stop The War Coalition planned to stage a series of protests in a bid to make its views known one last time before Bush left the world stage.

15th June, 2008

The Olympic Team GB medalists pose for the media as they arrive at Heathrow Airport from the 2008 Olympic Games in China, with a tally of 47 medals including 19 Golds.

25th August, 2008

The Publishers gratefully acknowledge Press Association Images, from whose extensive archive the photographs in this book have been selected. Personal copies of the photographs in this book, and many others, may be ordered online at www.prints.paphotos.com

**PRESS
ASSOCIATION
Images**

For more information, please contact:
Ammonite Press
AE Publications Ltd. 166 High Street, Lewes, East Sussex, BN7 1XU, United Kingdom
Tel: 01273 488005 Fax: 01273 402866
www.ammonitepress.com